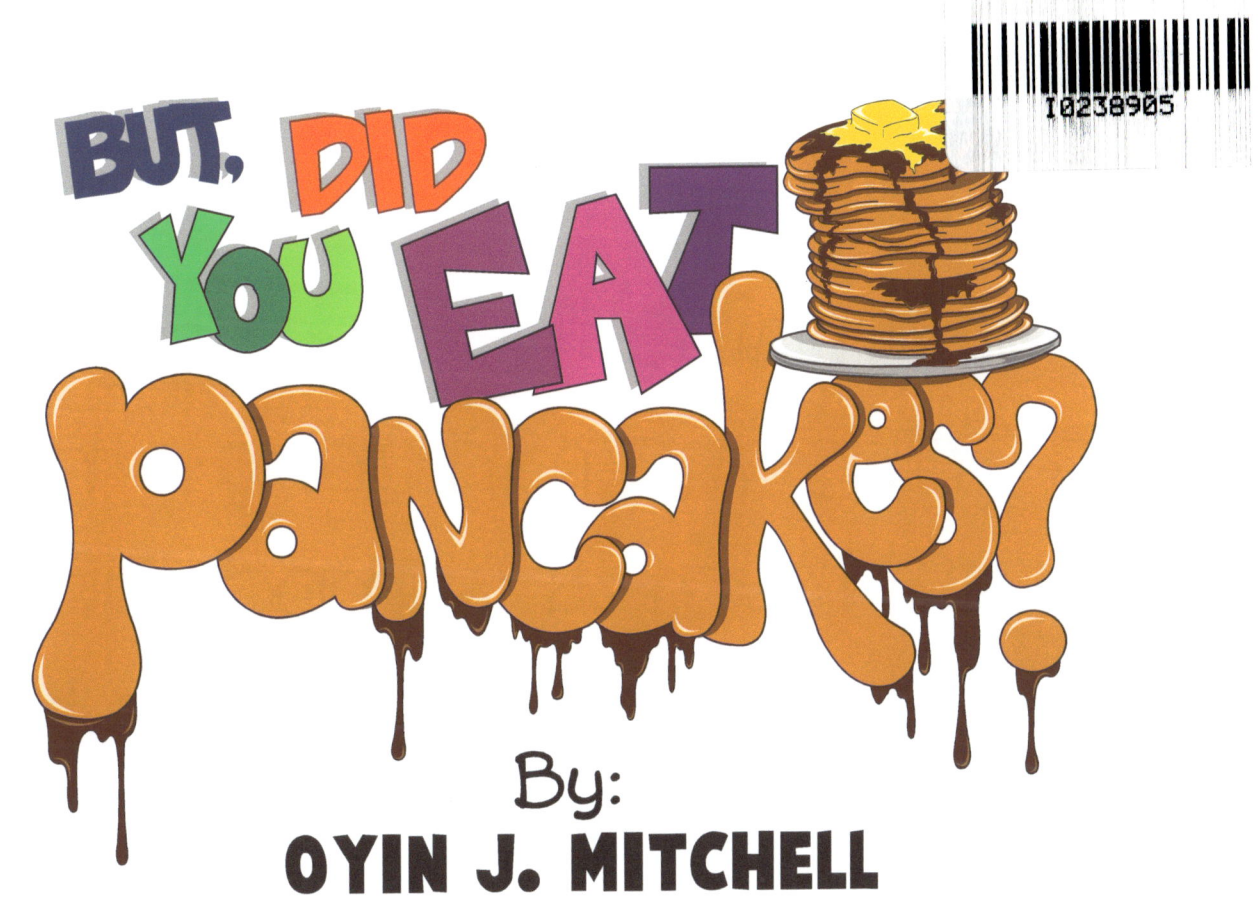

BUT, DID YOU EAT pancakes?

By:
OYIN J. MITCHELL

Co Author:
AJ MITCHELL

Illustrations by:
Lauren Lacy

A James & Jameson Company, LLC
A Publishing Company
Copyright 2020

Children find their identity by watching and mirroring others around them. It is important to know positive role models that look like them exist, so they never think that certain successes are for others only.

"Because there is always time for pancakes."
— AJ & Ava

It was 2:49 p.m. and as scheduled, bus 14-492 approached the driveway. Dad opened the front door just as the school bus came to a complete stop. AJ jumped off the bus with his little sister Ava not far behind, they both ran to the front door. He was excited to tell his parents about his black history assignment.

4.

5.

6.

AJ put his backpack on the table and pulled out his blue homework folder to get his assignment. The directions stated "Please choose and profile an African-American who has made a positive impact in the community." AJ's teacher, Mrs. K provided a list of suggestions for the class to choose.

Mom thought it would be a good idea to look for African Americans inside of the city they live in. She encouraged AJ to think about people who make meaningful contributions in Fayetteville, Georgia.

8.

AJ had an idea! He ran upstairs to his room and started searching his closet chest. He kept completed assignments from his previous school, Robin's Nest Preparatory Academy. AJ yelled, found it! He located the research assignment he completed for Mrs. Robin about the historic win of
Mayor 'Ed' Edward C. Johnson.

Together, AJ and Mom looked over the research and were surprised to learn that in the year of 2012 Mr. Johnson was elected to public office as a city councilman. In 2016, he served as the first African American mayor of Fayetteville. Before being elected to office, Mr. Johnson held a distinguished career of military service including serving as President of the Fayetteville NAACP chapter. He is head pastor of the oldest black church in Fayetteville Georgia, Flat Rock African Methodist Episcopal Church.
Mayor Johnson's achievements are historic and worthy of acknowledgement.

After AJ and Mom organized the plan, he and Dad began working on the finishing touches of the project. They created a portfolio of the historic election of Mayor Edward C. Johnson. Dad and AJ were proud of how they transformed a once plain poster into a professional portfolio.

The next day, AJ prepared to deliver his official presentation in class. He was dressed professionally, like a mayor, wearing a tie and suit jacket. He took a second look in the mirror, and thought, hmm...Mayor AJ? AJ was reminded the bus was coming in less than 5 minutes so he grabbed his project and headed out the front door.

Later in the month, Dad was reading the community newspaper, The Citizen. The local pancake house was hosting an event called *Pancakes and Politics* with Mayor Edward C. Johnson as the featured speaker.

Dad said "Hey AJ, looks like Mayor Johnson will be at the local pancake house next Saturday, it says he'll be giving a presentation about the new strategic plan for the city. Would you like to go? You never know, you may be able to meet him in person?" AJ excitedly replied, "Sure, go to the pancake house? I'd love it because I LOVE pancakes."

On Saturday morning, AJ jumped out of bed, brushed his teeth, and put on his clothes. He yelled "Mom are you almost ready? I don't want to be late because I am ready to eat pancakes ! Is it ok if I wait in the car?"

Mom replied, "go ahead and get in the car, I'm right behind you. We want to be on time so we don't miss the mayor's presentation."

Ava stayed home to practice for the taping of her weekly Youtube Show, "The Ava Show."
AJ's little sister is so creative, friendly, loves to dance and talk, talk, and yes, talk. Before mom and AJ left, Ava reminded him, "don't forget to eat lots of pancakes."

AJ and Mom arrived at the pancake house just in time to hear the mayor. The restaurant was filled with people- standing room only to be exact. Everyone was attentive in listening to the exciting news about plans for the city of Fayetteville. Waitresses carried plates as the smell of coffee permeated the air and yes pancakes were almost on every table! Unfortunately, there was nowhere for AJ and his mom to sit.

28.

29.

30.

The two of them stood in the back of the room and waited for an open seat. They saw a hand waving in the air, it was Aunt Shannon! AJ ran over to sit on her lap and he too started attentively listening to the mayor give his presentation about the city's plan.

AJ looked in amazement because he had never seen anything like this before, there were so many people packed in the restaurant eating and listening to the words of Mayor Johnson. The event was also being live-streamed on social media for anyone to participate if they couldn't attend in person.

34.

Meanwhile, Mom spoke with one of the event organizers and after the mayor finished his presentation he came over to meet AJ in person, just like dad said. Both Mayor Johnson and AJ were all smiles as he reached up and gave the mayor a big hug!

AJ opened his project to show his work and grade of 100%.
Mayor Johnson looked over the details right in the pancake house. The mayor later took pictures with AJ and his mom.
AJ and Mayor Johnson chatted about his school Cleveland Elementary, his second grade teacher Mrs. K, and his love for math.

38.

Meeting Mayor Johsnon made AJ so
happy it's all he talked to his
mom about during the ride home.
He couldn't wait to
tell his little sister and dad about it.

AJ and Mom arrived home from Pancakes and Politics at about 1:00 o'clock in the afternoon. Just as AJ started to share his experience about meeting Mayor Johnson, his little sister Ava politely interrupted and said "that's great that you met the mayor, but did you eat pancakes?"

41.

42.

AJ realized,
" OH NO! I forgot to eat pancakes!"

After Dad and AJ prepared the batter, they served pancakes for the family to enjoy!